we, the monstrous

script for an unrealizable film

mark ducharme

the operating system c. 2018

the operating system print//document chapbook

we, the monstrous

ISBN: 978-1-946031-41-9
Library of Congress Control Number: 2018945769
copyright © 2018 by Mark DuCharme
edited and designed by Lynne DeSilva-Johnson with poetry editor Peter Milne Greiner

is released under a Creative Commons CC-BY-NC-ND (Attribution, Non Commercial, No Derivatives) License: its reproduction is encouraged for those who otherwise could not afford its purchase in the case of academic, personal, and other creative usage from which no profit will accrue. Complete rules and restrictions are available at: http://creativecommons.org/licenses/by-nc-nd/3.0/
For additional questions regarding reproduction, quotation, or to request a pdf for review contact operator@theoperatingsystem.org

This text was set in The Constellation of Heracles, Minion, Hand Printing Press Stencil, and OCR-A Standard. Books from The Operating System are distributed to the trade by SPD/Small Press Distribution, with ePub and POD via Ingram, with production by Spencer Printing, in Honesdale, PA, in the USA.

Cover Art uses a photo of boxers Cal Delaney and Johnny Kilbane, in a photo from the Bain News Service taken between 1910 and 1915. It is available in the public domain, from the George Grantham Bain Collection.

The operating system is a member of the Radical Open Access Collective, a community of scholar-led, not-for-profit presses, journals and other open access projects. Now consisting of 40 members, we promote a progressive vision for open publishing in the humanities and social sciences.
Learn more at: http://radicaloa.disruptivemedia.org.uk/about/

Your donation makes our publications, platform and programs possible! We <3 You.
bit.ly/growtheoperatingsystem

the operating system
141 Spencer Street #203
Brooklyn, NY 11205
www.theoperatingsystem.org
operator@theoperatingsystem.org

we, the monstrous

script for an unrealizable film

mark ducharme

"And we'll produce history as others produce plays." —Herzog

Author's Note:

The three acts are rather different,
if also interlinked parts of a whole,
and should be filmed or staged thus,
so that their contrast & incongruity are heightened.

DRAMATIS PERSONNAE

SHE / PLATONESSE / THE FINAL GIRL
HE / BÉRANGER
WHITE NOISE
THE CHORUS
THE MOB
THE DIRECTOR
SPECTATOR 1
SPECTATOR 2
SPECTATOR 3
SPECTATOR 4
THE SECURITY FORCES
A SERVANT
NARRATOR*

*All unattributed lines may be spoken by the narrator, or perhaps by a variety of narrators, a harmony or cacophony.

ACT I

scene one

There is a blindspot from which   the camera   cannot see
Only the strange   suggestion   of a person   in the foreground
A mirror linked to   visibly   as your own reaction   ~~shot~~
    To the 24-hour disaster news cycle

Hidden   under the shapes of trees   which have no music
But smell   like ancient hands   encompassing flowers
Or the purple suggestion   of a woman's hair   pulled back
    Which somehow   is like synaesthesia
       Or the darker notes of our voices in the rain

———

SCENE: Everything is in it. It is painted, mirrored, brutal, like the republican national convention, but it does not bear any names. Everyone lives in a national purgatory quite unaware of the eyes studying, studying each other, in order to meet. In order to be in this house. (Pause for national anthem.) To specifically dwell. Do my own eyes look frantic? Outside the vermillion pavilion where all the extras (a cast of tens of thousands) have lost their shirts. Their navy blue blazers with pinkish or red or fuchsia or bright blue or darker blue or glaring, purplish ties with American-flag clips. *Which the dead cannot answer for.* ~~Can the dead hear this?~~

———

The scene is what clouds the appearance
It is a necessary rupture

As pedestrians cough at the force of suggestion
& The yellow moon is private

Chortling for attention
While deep in the tracking shot
The scene writhes, lacking continuity

The scene is a specific focus,
A narrow room or building

The scene lacks infrastructure, except by the
Producer's sudden grace

Which is old & foreign as pop bottles
Signaling a breakdown in the commercial imagination

The chase scene must be a force of nature
Else it's just a waste of film

Which crumples & decays, then burns
In idle
Myths of Hollywood's sidewalks

As a coat sways elegantly in the breeze
Fur coat, hung on fence— faded glamour— cut scene

scene two

[It has all already happened. THE CHORUS enters, dejectedly.]

C: There is no freedom
Against hope
Which soon
Falls away

In the clear of
Postmodern lies
& In the ruins of
What we despise—

Where empty
Telling now consumes,
Deludes, then soon
Becomes

The speaker—
Who steals our very
Breath &
Chatter—

& The good we can't
Even remember
If still we almost knew—
Ever after,

Ever af-
ter, ev-
er af-
ter.

[THE MOB's shouts can be heard from far away. They grow louder & louder. Enter THE MOB.]

M: The government is dead now!
It burns like a figleaf!

Let democracy's pyre
Burn brighter & brighter

Into this strange
New day—

& Welcome *White*
Noise, *White*

Noise, *White*
Noise!—

The engine of our chaos,
The fire to our pillars which consumes

Everything we would not wish
To tell—

The Honcho who's going to get things done
Even if he has to kill

Everyone
& Every livid thing.

O White Noise— come,
See what you've won!

[Sound of cheers. Deafening. WHITE NOISE enters, buoyed by the MOB. Fake smile, blankly waved greetings. In the distance, hints of smoke, fire & ruin. Reporters on the scene, plastic-haired, blathering, cannot be heard.]

scene three

[There are only two people speaking. There only ever are.]

SHE: I dreamed rhinoceroses dancing,
    Burning up the streets.

HE: I don't know if there is anything here
    For us to lay bare.

SHE: There is no 'us.' Collective
    Agency has been destroyed,
    Made suspect by the forms
    Of narrative & history.

HE: History is just a way
    To organize the past. It is
    Only another narrative
    Like (or unlike) ours.

SHE: The past no longer exists
    If it ever did.
    Actually, I'm not interested in
    The past. People
    Don't *say things* when they speak.
    Speech is emotional, trans-
    actional, irrational, but seldom
    Functional, but in the most
    Mundane & easy ways.

HE: Speech is a dream
    We've woken up to.

SHE: If we've woken,
        How would we know? & If we're speaking,
            That implies
        A listener— so is it *speech*, when we talk
        To ourselves?

HE: Everyone is usually
        Alone, but mostly
        Speaking.

SHE: Exactly. & So what does speech
        Do, except allow the speaker
        To hear her- or himself?
        It is an echo, proving we're still here.

HE: Like dreams, in that sense, which are
        Thought's energy continuing
        Once consciousness
        Has left.

SHE: Yet the meaning of dreams is
        Hidden, though one senses it is
        There, whereas
                We take for granted
        Speech's meanings, yet they are
        Received, transient, inconsequent-
            ial, fleeting. A touch or a look
        Often says more.

HE: But you can *say*
Anything you want to, presumably—
So is the problem speech or the
Speaker?

SHE: Both. Neither. You could say
The problem is *us*. *We* is a culture
Unreflective, lazy, in-
fantilized by pretty
Glowing screens.

HE: Hence your own dream,
Yes?

SHE: Oh, I haven't read that play.
& It was written before cellphones &
Tablets, before social media &
The disenfranchisement of
Journalism. Anyway,
   What's the point of reading
When the world's about to
Burn away?

HE: The world was
On fire, then as now.

SHE: The world is *always*
On fire. Only the victims change.

HE: The oppressors do not change.
They remain an image of the monstrous.

SHE: No, they are an image of
    Ourselves— of what humanity,
    Our *species*,
        Is capable of doing.
    Humans behave inhumanly,
    Inhu*mane*ly, instinctively, & then *define*
        Ourselves, a species, as
    The opposite of all our actions.

HE: That is a dark view of our collective
    Selves.

SHE: It is the only one that history
    Allows.— Our selves are neither
  'Dark' nor 'light'
      But fully bright, illumined
    In the glare of what
    Debord called the spectacle.

HE: That 'spectacle' is all we have.

SHE: Yet it is always, fully, up for grabs.

scene four

[THE CHORUS, *still dejected, speaks.*]

> The year is ending   & we   we were never here
> Year was a trap   engulfing us
>   In forms of noise   while headlines burst &
> Everything everything screams
>
>   She is right— the voice
> No matter what one says
>   Is a fiction
>   A transmission
> An act of faith in sound's coherence
> & That words are less   but also more
>   More than we take
>   Them to be

[THE DIRECTOR, *screaming now off-camera*]

> *Whose* voice? *Whose* sense of loss?
> *Whose* very land grown foreign
> Not by strangers but those too familiar?
> *Whose* delivery? *Whose* lines?
> *Whose* uncanniness? *Whose* hate &
> Empathy? Whose hate? Whose
> Hate   whose hate   whose
> Hate?

[the CHORUS, as in a Greek tragedy]

        The voice you choose
        Is your own construction—
        A mirror laughing at
        All the forms that silence takes
        While this very sentence
        Burns the page.—

scene five

[The DIRECTOR continues speaking. Sometimes he won't shut up. He is seen on camera as a shadow behind a screen. He has an unmistakable air of self-importance.]

>The film is about the eye
>The screenplay, about the word
>
>Where do words & eyes meet
>When light arrives
>In unwritten sleep?
>
>What images
>Do you let roll in?
>
>What light   what light
>Do you squander
>When the sun is about to die?
>
>The pictured is captured—
>A flicker
>
>Of light on pale
>Blue screen
>
>Against which all
>Performance quakes
>
>(It's the screens we watch,
>Not actors)
>
>Grown slender
>As the weathered
>
>Dreams
>
>Of love we occupy

scene six

The voice is monstrous. It is the rhythm of what's left onscreen consciousness's debris ~~what the monstrous brings to the party~~ it's snowing in the world somewhere the heat of the sun through the window on my face ~~where the world shuts down~~ Scene: there are people milling about the world is uncertain & the streets the streets rustle with an implied violence ~~violence is always just underneath possibility's horizon~~ an old man is walking talking to himself there is a *scream* a sense of light changing light goes past everything is immediate The Clash's "Hate and War" is playing for some reason swathes of light & someone someone is selling something calling prices out this is the only human voice one hears ~~the spoken is unclean~~ light flickers down a bay or river a nondescript body of water brought in to reflect the light the camera pans spins catches fire at one point in its sharp gyrations everyone is old suddenly old & the world the world's old without wisdom all squandered & the word rings then appears.

———

Sun burns up
Night's debris
The scene is a pier
Crowded with boats

Water burning oil
Tankers dutifully
Rigged
Colossal as night in the dreary dawn rain

The interrupted
Narrative
Burns

In memory's
Dying
Kiss

ACT II

scene one

[HE & SHE meet another day. HE at first seems to be talking to himself & doesn't seem to see her]

HE: I liked that book rather better
      After reading it than during
                    The process.—

SHE *(interjecting, as if irritated)*:
      I told you, I don't read.

HE: O, you're right. Sorry.—
      Hey, I heard your name was Joan.

SHE: I think from now on I'll call you Bérenger.

HE: Hearing is not real. That was your point about speech, wasn't it?

SHE: I can't remember the past. Now I am old. Now I am young,
      Now both & the same.

HE: As old as dying laughter.

SHE: Now you sound like a poet. You ought to be ashamed!

HE: Art thou Plato?

SHE: Rather, Platonesse.

HE: O, free me of this double-speak!

SHE: Hear yourself— thine only double;
      Hear laughter burn while history quakes.

[A TV comes on— TVs are always doing that— & a speech by WHITE NOISE dimly can be seen & heard, though his words are indiscernible.]

[PLATONESSE— for she has been given a name— stares at the screen for a few moments pitilessly, then turns to the camera.]

      In this Will to Madness
      All future's lost
      As the year turns young again

      What will we know? & Where the name
      For this grave at the end of song
      With a voice stuck in history's ache?

      In the mirror where we don't
      Know how to speak
      At this mirror where we don't

      & Speak, in ashes, blurts &
      Non sequiturs & unreflective
      Noise

      While the pain born in living
      Eats at our selves
      Burns our unrepentant songs & prayers

Catches us in winter's throat—
You can't leave the pain   can't
Shut it away

Awake to beauty
In our dread
While the earth turns to paper

Crumpled   torn
& Winter burns
Its mysterious ash

To wreck this song
In its monster thoughts & fears
& Fertilize the stolen

scene two

[WHITE NOISE speaks. Everywhere people are chanting & jeering. Fires sporadically are started, windows broken, women & children pelted with stones, the elderly trampled & beaten, LGBTQ people brutalized.]

When, in grace to be unbothered
Spectators & followers
Emotion junkies who seethe
In the very act of misnaming
Misattributing & mistaking
The least for the most
Corporate for corporeal
Transience for the eternal
Grave for womb
In the fear that flowers in so many
In conformity-comfort
With a silver spoon up the rear
Or a good American plastic one— o
See can you swear
By the little you care
& All ye fear
& By night's stark rumors
That greed may go on
& The sun
Fall away
Into mourning's new day
& The rich get away
Ever after
Ever after
Ever after

[THE MOB takes up the chant inconsolably.]

> Ever after!
> Ever after!
> Ever after!

SPECTATOR 1:
> But what about me?
> Where will my glory be?

WHITE NOISE:
> Your glory, madame, is in supporting *me*!

[Sound of laughter, perhaps from THE MOB, perhaps canned.]

SPECTATOR 2:
> What about me?
> I cannot see.

WHITE NOISE:
> Then you are my favorite supporter of all!

SPECTATOR 3:
> What about me? What about me?
> I'm of a race you'll never be.

WHITE NOISE:
> Take that man out & have him mauled!

[The SECURITY FORCES enter & forcibly drag SPECTATOR 3 away. Sound of vicious dogs growling & barking off camera. Later, sound of human screams.]

SPECTATOR 4:
>   Free that man from his plight!
>   Just because you're El Honcho doesn't give you the right!

WHITE NOISE:
>   Seize that traitor! Seize that traitor!
>   Show her just what dissenters are in for!

*[The MOB turns on SPECTATOR 4. They become like rabid **Maenads** at an ancient Dionysian rite. They tear SPECTATOR 4 to shreds. Blood & strips of flesh are everywhere. Somebody captures it on cellphone camera, but the SECURITY FORCES come smash the phone & brutalize its owner. The plastic-haired reporters, the few who haven't already gotten their sound bytes, flee in terror. Fires rage in the distance & smoke bellows, drowning out the image as screams are drowned in the rhythm of THE MOB's incessant chanting.]*

scene three

[It is a few days later. THE CHORUS speaks.]

In the language of stark flowers
All eyes meet
& We go up the street
People dance
It is a celebration— because one must either mourn or rejoice
There is hardly ever anything between

& We walk, refusing
To be idle
To just sit idly by
In the wind with noses broken

Broken, fractured in
The dark
In the dark where we came from
Which named us
Consumes us
As everything you've dreamed learned & forgotten

This isn't a voice
It's Poetry, a body
A body you came from
In the wind not telling

Wind doesn't tell
All of her sources
Her deep diversions
Her unnamable cries

Which fill our hearts with chatter
As the beholden grow dim

While the room & all its sources
Lay bare what's happening
In acts of violence
In the moment being seen

The moment is not true
It's savage, but too real
In the thrill of night's delivery
Hungry with savage voices

Which daylight fears, & where
All hungry monsters loom
Sick with ravished bravado
But thirsting—

Thirsting for your peace.

scene four

[BÉRANGER— *for He, too, has been given a name*— & WHITE NOISE *meet. Because He is Béranger, he is also drunk.*]

WN: I am everything & I am beautiful.
    I wish you weren't here.

B: What do wishes matter?
    I shall address myself to the crowd.

WN: The crowd has been ordered away.
    I own the rights to public discourse now.
    I could sell you shares
    At top dollar.

B: To sell or buy
    The common good,
    Something of infinite value,
    With what is merely an agreed upon idea,
    Though a rank & filthy one.

WN: My money is beauty
    Itself— & if you haven't noticed
    I've already poisoned your 'common good,'
    Polluted public discourse,
    Raped rhetoric, shitted on science.

B: Why am I even talking to you,
    You void in search of a self;
    You swirl of clangor; you swiller
    Of lies & all that's most reptilian;

You inhuman replica of refuse in human guise;
You rank liar; you foul, mendacious sludge;
You dissembler who would disassemble
All that's left that's fine & true & real,
Honest & compassionate. You'd raze
The very bones of our democracy & sell
Them for scraps— you beggar
For attention in cheap rhetoric;
You buzzard; you grabber for whom nothing or no one's inviolable;
You blank stain on our history, our
Consciousness & all our knowing;
You piece of trash picked up in a casino by a Mafioso;
You middleman; you grubber for landlessness;
You seller of what none dare own nor buy;
You cheap hood in a business suit;
You scrap of nothing no one's ever named.

WN: I hear 'me' in your speech. I like that.

B: You hear your own voice
In a drunkard's shitting.

WN: *You're* a drunkard!

B: Only because I have to
Interact with
You
    In real historical time.

WN: Nothing is real.

B: That's where you're wrong.
      Love & hatred are real.
      A baby's finger's grasp is real.
      Our changing climate— real.
      A city, a kiss or a flower— all real.
      It's only *you* who are not real.
      You're a simulacrum, a storyboard
      Written for cameras with no film.
      You're love with no object, passion
      Without purpose— for you
      Only love yourself & your own kind;
      & You're hatred with no bounds, for there's
      No 'other' with whom you can empathize.

WN: O, I am real alright.
      I can destroy like no other
      Monster, hunger or ghost-
      Of-a-thing.
      & I am reason's nightmare:
      The abiding need which does not care.

B: You are all of that, & more—
      & Yes you can do great, great harm.
      Yet for all of that, for all
      That power, you're still a pathetic, fearful child
      Pleasing only himself,
      Waiting for the wide world to raise him
      To something so much larger,
      So much greater than he is—
      Nostalgia for a glory
      That cannot be, nor ever was.

WN *(enraged)*:
    Guards! Seize this man!
    Have my scientists— the best ones—
    Turn him to an elephant,
    For elephants are so docile, &
    You can poach their tusks for ivory,
    Which is a great source of income.

B *(being dragged away)*:
    If I'm turned into an elephant,
    I'll only gore you like a giant bull!

WN *(to lackeys, who may or may not be there)*:
    Assemble all my brokers & my whores;
    I've already broken down the door!

ACT III

scene one

[PLATONESSE, alone in an abandoned oilfield. Ruin & destruction abound.]

    P: What's this? Barely had I settled in
          To pray or to think or to Tweet
          When news is brought to me
          That the one we shall call Béranger
          Has been taken by the state,
          Arrested, on the charge
          That, being now a drunkard,
          He is of a foreign nationality.

          O vile fate! I sort of liked that guy,
          & I do not want to see the poor,
          Reckless slob imprisoned!
          Yet what can I do? For the king—
          I mean, El Presidente,
          That rank honcho, our kleptocrat—
          Has seized poor Béranger.

          But that's the way it's got to stay.
          So let's begin a new day—
          Hip hop hurray!
          Now if you'll excuse me, folks, I have to check my *Twitter*.

THE CHORUS (*entering, stage left*):
          You'd do as well to look in a toilet,
          For you'll find as much of value there.

P: Who are you— a gang of thugs
   Come to pillage all I own?

C: Calm down, Platonesse. You've had
   The power all along—
   Not 'ruby slippers' exactly,
   But the capacity to distinguish right
   From wrong, if not quite the courage
   To do very much about it.

P: What can I do? I'm only me—
   A woman of color & of
   Fertility's age.

C: We all can do something, & you
   Have the gift of insight,
   Although you do not see or use it
   Very well.

P: My gifts are my own business—
   But you haven't answered the question: why
   Have you come to anger me?

C: We have answered, but you haven't
   Listened. We've come to tell
   You that *you* have the power—
   Not that bullshit 'superhero' power
   You see
           In movies & on TV,
   Which is fake— a false reality

To accompany fake news.
Your power is of a different degree—
You can discern love from hate,
Truth from nonsense, lies from what
We can breathe & touch & feel & see.

P: I do not feel, but that
    I have to go
    Now to bake,
    Or watch, or do
    Any other thing
    But that which would lead
    Me to a dismal
    End
    At the hands of that predator-president
    For whom even truth does bend.

C: A straight line bends the crooked truth.

P: Now you appease me with veiled mockery!

C: It is history we mock.

P: It's only history because we make it.

C: That's a lie & you know it;
    The past lives here
    Among us, as palpable as all that sand
    You see round, as if it still led up
    To old Ozymandias's tomb.

P: O, do not swarm my head with your fine words!—
      The world is wicked & the truth in shards.
      Let me go now, to be among my kin
      Who, being humans, no such truths have seen.

C: Get away, then, & wash thy hands!
      See no blood on them, Mortal, for it isn't comely
      & It bears diseases, bonds, similitude,
      & This last, perhaps, is what frightens
      Most. To help anyone's to have seen a ghost;
      Safety's at stake in the twilit air,
      & Security's a heavy world to bear—
          A cross on fire
          When things get dire.

[CHORUS starts to exit, heads heavy.]

P (*torn, hesitates at first*):
      Wait, wait! I'll do your deed.
      I'll take up the pact which truth does need.
      I'll enter the chamber which chills my bones.
      I'll even be with that— *thing*— all alone!
      I will risk my breath & chill my bones
      In order to bring poor Béranger home.
      & If I can't, or even perish
      My bones will know this is not finished.

scene two

[WHITE NOISE, *strutting about in his chamber. The walls are filled with wide TV screens, each silently showing a different 'feed.' Jarring distraction & pontification.*]

>WN: My beauty is money, & when I go to bed
>Visions of emptiness swarm my head.
>I'm the most powerful fool in the hemisphere;
>I am the blight of which you feared.
>My palaces are the finest eyesores,
>My drones the best with which you're gored.
>Everything is perfect about me except you,
>You Other, who couldn't buy one of my shoes
>Which I'd sell at top dollar. I sell everything thus,
>Except health, air, water, dignity, & such.

[*The camera cuts to PLATONESSE, who is crawling through a tunnel of barbed wire to get to WHITE NOISE's chamber. She is clothed in armor, yet still cuts herself from time to time. Blood smears with streaming sweat. She grits her teeth. She carries or is wearing a machete & a spear. It is in this shot, which probably lasts for several minutes, that PLATONESSE is transformed into THE FINAL GIRL.*]

[*The scene returns to WHITE NOISE's chamber.*]

>WN: I am all of beauty
>& The poor's death cries.
>
>THE FINAL GIRL (*entering through an air vent near the ceiling which she kicks open with her boots, leaping to the floor*):
>
>Shit is prettier than you, White Noise.

WN: Guards! Who are you, Intruder?

FG: They are all distracted by their *Twitter* feeds
    & Reruns of reality TV.
    They will do you no good now. As for me,
    I am a woman of color,
    So my identity,
    My selfhood, should hardly matter to you,
    You, my racist kindred.

WN: I have no black relatives; look up my tree.

FG: Yet aren't we all one species?
    & This is perhaps what sickens me
    Most about you— that I have to
    Live with & confront the fact
    That there are those of my 'kind'
    Who can so easily turn their backs
    On their fellows, & all creation.

WN: Ha!
    I know you as an atheist!

FG: It's easiest to do evil
    When you're convinced you are one of the 'good.'
    Yet it's the self-professed righteous who mostly do
    Wrong, with a little help from the bitterly
    Entitled.— You, for instance.

WN: I love everyone who does love me.

FG: That is many more than I might have guessed,
    But still far too few to make a country.

WN: A country is what I make
    & Just what it takes.

FG: You who've never made anything
    But on the bones of labor & slaves
    Would dare that claim?

WN: Listen, doll, I'll say anything
    I want.

FG (*looking him in the eye, clutching her weapons, & lowering her voice fiercely*):

Don't you
Ever
Call me
Doll!

WN: I'll say anything
    If it profits me, &
    Much of it does: doll
    Doll doll doll!

FG: Your litany distracts
    From any, much less all the facts.

WN: The facts are trash.

FG: Only if you want to twist the truth
To suit the devil's purpose.

WN: I'm going to ban the truth;
It will be beauty itself.

FG: "Beauty is truth, truth beauty."

WN: Who said that? I'll lock him up.

FG: He's been dead for nearly 200 years.

WN: Then I'll have my people confiscate his tomb.

FG: There are some things none can ever own.

WN: O, *I* can own *anything*—
Just look what I've done!

FG: You haven't done anything
But the habits you've rung up.

WN: Who told you about that?

FG: Certainly not the media—
But I have my methods, &
They suit me.

WN: How can that be?
     The media hate me.

FG: Everyone loves a powerful laughingstock.

WN: Guards! Seize this freak!

FG: I've already told you— there are none.

WN: O no! Will you pull off my hair?

FG: I have no interest in what's under there.

WN: What then, what then will you do?

FG: Aguirre, my kindred, I have come to kill you.

WN: I can give you 2 million in bullion tomorrow.
     There's a ship that's leaving town.

FG: I won't be on that ship.

WN: Then what's your trip?

FG: I want to see Béranger
     Brought here alive
     In this very room by the 'morrow
     Else your very breath will be your sorrow.

WN: I own all breath
     Including yours.

          I'll sell you shares
          Or you can do my chores.

FG: Not until
          My own breath is lost
          Shall I buy from you anything,
          Even at cost.

WN: You drive a hard bargain.

FG: Your thoughts are clogged with jargon.

WN: What am I to do?

FG: Béranger, Béranger, now, I say!

WN: What? When there's so much yet to do—
          Despoiling earth, commoditizing
          Human need & love & suffering
          In the holy name of greed?

FG: Nothing is holy from thy unholy face
          Which shrivels rapture & burns up grace.

WN: Guards!— O yeah, you told me.
          Hey, listen— why don't you join me?
          I can make you an icon, even a saint;
          You'll have all the best.
          Nothing your eyes see
          Ever will rust.

FG: Except for you & your privileged spew
 Which would ransom all life for the perishing few.

WN: Then what can I do?

FG: Take me to Béranger or bring him here
 Unless you want me to chop off your hair.

WN: My hair! My hair! O don't go there!

FG: Then bring him, bring him, bring him here!

WN *(calling out)*:
 O unarmed, dusky servant,
 Bring me the poor, shackled recluse
 Whose horrid crime is calumny.

[SERVANT *enters, head bowed, bringing along with her* BÉRANGER, *who's almost naked, now emaciated.* BÉRANGER *looks worse than Antonin Artaud did after receiving over fifty electroshock treatments.* THE FINAL GIRL *gasps to see* BÉRANGER *thus.* WHITE NOISE *throws change on the floor which the* SERVANT *scoops up hungrily, like a Third World peasant.* SERVANT *exits quickly.*]

FG: O vilest thing of woman born.
 O death for whom there is no tomb
 Filthy enough to accommodate
 Your rank greed, your brazen need.

WN: I need everything because I'm me.
 The future is an oligarchy.
 The past doesn't matter because it's shattered.

>   Ha ha! I've won—
>   Your fine ideas are a burnt-out sun.

[THE FINAL GIRL's jaw clenches. She stares her nemesis in the eye pitilessly, coldly, fiercely. WHITE NOISE, for the first time, truly looks frightened. THE FINAL GIRL brandishes her spear.]

> FG: O no, not yet—
>   Not 'til you've met
>   Your fate & let it wither you
>   Shall our appointment
>   Yet be through!

[THE FINAL GIRL thrusts her spear into WHITE NOISE's heart. Methane spews from his heart, mouth & anus. THE FINAL GIRL thrusts her weapon into WHITE NOISE's belly, & methane spews from there as well. No blood ever drops & no tears fall.]

> WN *(seriously wounded, staggering)*:
>   What's this I see? What's this I see?
>   My beauty's slipping out of me!
>   The air smells like money
>   But I cannot harvest its bounty
>   So I'll die all alone—
>   In this tower, my tomb!

[THE FINAL GIRL kicks one of his legs out from under him. He falls, & with her spear she now delivers his final blow, impaling him. WHITE NOISE is dead.]

[BÉRANGER, who has been quietly fading all this time, groans. THE FINAL GIRL turns to him.]

FG: O Béranger, dear, are you alright?

B: I fear, Platonesse, I won't see one more night.

FG *(tearing)*:
O Béranger, Béranger, there's so much to say.

B: There's no time for that now, & there never was.

FG: But I've killed the tyrant;
The beast is vanquished.

B: Yes, but that's not to say it's finished.

FG: But he lies there lifeless & cold as fear.
Can you not see that, Béranger dear?

B: Look, look! What spews from his putrid corpse?
It is all the living fear the most.

FG: That smell that exudes from his bloated ass
The winds will move. It will quickly pass.

B: No, no, you are wrong! It is much worse.
It ruins love & pollutes the earth.
It burdens climate & breeds our fears.
It burns everything that has ever been here.

FG: Dead I said, & dead he is.
The tyrant can no more befoul us.

B *(fading, looking worse by the moment)*:
    But that's where you're wrong—
    The deed is done,
    The poisoned cup already tasted,
    All love & good will already wasted.

[BÉRANGER gasps. He struggles to say more, but cannot. His head drops lifeless to the floor. He is dead. THE FINAL GIRL is mute in shock & grief. Tears well in her eyes. THE CHORUS enters.]

C: You've killed El Honcho. There's nothing left.
      Now his men will come for your very breath.
      We know we encouraged you, but we have to run.
      More blood will likely end this song.

[THE CHORUS scatters like cockroaches in a kitchen when the light's turned on.]

FG *(looking frightened, quickly locks the door behind them, then goes to the window & looks out. Tears stream down her face. She pauses, but when she finally speaks her tone is firm & somber, as if suddenly resigned to her fate)*:

    They're right. The security forces come
    Winding up the path of stone!
    Soon all will be done, & the ruin
    Which Béranger foretold
    In his dying breath will befoul the earth
    While the hearts of men grow cold.—

    But that smell— I know it! That gas leaching
    From the tyrant's rotting corpse
    Is methane rising, rising up

Like a ghost of his enmity,
High up, high up, until it wipe
All sustenance from the sky.—

But the prophecy— there was something more
My dying *frère* foretold:
If good will's lost, then love itself
& Human decency;
Can our land have lost so much from just
This tin despot's ascendancy?
Have bitterness, mistrust & fear
Replaced all in common we once held dear?
Have love & empathy been soiled by greed
& The noxious epithets we've been fed?
Has the very blood from our veins been sold
For false comfort & gilded homes?—

But what is that noise? The things are here!
Soon they'll have torn down the door.
I'll not be brutalized like Béranger;
There is still yet another way!

[PLATONESSE *takes her machete and slashes her own throat. She slowly drops to the floor &, as the thrashing at the door grows ever louder, she fades and dies. After some time & more, ever louder sounds of thrashing, the door bursts open. Enter* THE CHORUS.]

C: Platonesse, you won't believe it!
The security forces have disbanded
& Many a soldier has joined our fight;
The government is now like a cobra headless;
Senators flee their offices in fright.

Already a crowd grows in the square
Chanting your name & wanting to hear
Your words of hope & bravery,
Those qualities lost but now redeemed.

What's this? The heroine who killed
The tyrant now sleeps in her own blood pooled!
What fate is this that can't release
All our souls from their crushing grief?
Take down the banners & the flags;
Replace them all with coal-black rags
& Mourn not just this infamy
But also the death of what we wanted to be.
It shall not come easily. It shall not
Come easily. Get now
To the streets & sing;
With songs of resistance let the monuments ring.
With this death, let us be reborn
'Til love & liberty awake from their tomb!

afterword

A script is only a *potential* work. And though I call this work a "script" in its subtitle, *We, the Monstrous* is a work of poetry. If Ezra Pound famously defined the epic as a "poem including history," then this work is a poem that *takes place in* history. And if that move seems counter to Pound's politically and poetically, so much the better.

The allusion to Eugène Ionesco's *Rhinoceros*, which some will note, felt necessary not for that author's association with Theater of the Absurd precisely. I read that play as an allegory of resistance and complicity during the rise of 20th century fascism. Thus, I take it as a touchstone for the kind of art that might be made, that perhaps must be made, during the present moment of historical struggle. Ionesco makes his fascist collaborators put on rhinoceros heads; I make mine equally faceless— the Mob in this work is contrasted with the more sympathetic, if equally faceless, Chorus. However, while for the purposes of dramatic action the Mob here is a "faceless crowd," there is an important difference: as Platonesse points out, that crowd is *us*. Thus, when she takes on her role as The Final Girl, the (mythic?) monster she goes to slay, like some latter-day Greek hero(ine), must be seen in some sense as a version of herself, as well as a version of me and you, or of what we might be, what we might have become, despite our assurances to ourselves, despite our sense of being justified and "good." I feel it's especially important to stress, at this moment where the United States is so profoundly, perhaps irrevocably, divided, that hatred, racism and avarice are not traits of the Others; they are, tragically, *human* traits as surely as are compassion, love, empathy and generosity. In this sense, but *only* so, my unwitting protagonist Platonesse at least partially speaks for me. And like us and also like Ionesco's protagonist, she must ultimately decide whether she will accept the darker human traits— and *yes*, conformity and obedience *are* dark traits, especially in the face of nascent autocracy— or actively resist them.

I felt it very important to have a protagonist who was in no way an "alter ego" of myself; thus, Platonesse insists that she does not read, even as she seems at least somewhat familiar with Debord's *La Societé du Spectacle*, the Ionesco play (which again she protests she has not read), and even Plato's *Republic*. (When my character Béranger— not to be confused with his namesake, the protagonist of Ionesco's play— somewhat jokingly accuses her of being

Plato in response to her condemnation of his "[sounding] like a poet," she doesn't flinch, nor is she confused at the reference, but instead takes on the mantle of a kind of ironically empowered female heir to Plato. Of course, in so doing, she unwittingly takes on the role of determining who should be or have voice in the Republic— and here her condemnation ultimately centers not on poets but on a certain other character, sometimes referred to as the "Honcho" or "Presidente." It is this figure who is the most immediate danger to the Republic, despite Platonesse's teasing of Béranger.)

Regarding the character of White Noise, some will be tempted to read him as simply representing one contemporary political figure. While there are resemblances, certainly, it would be a mistake to read him as merely or even primarily representing this individual. White Noise, instead, represents the hatred, greed, racism and white privilege manifest in US culture circa 2017— something that is much larger than this individual, and without which this person, in his present state, would not even exist. (This is why, when White Noise is killed, his body does not bleed but instead emits methane. Methane, in this sense, of course represents the very real danger to the climate which unwise energy policies pose; however, besides being a reference to the poisoning of our literal atmosphere, methane here is also a metaphor for the poisoning of our *cultural* atmosphere. White Noise, thus, is not only a man but an idea— and a very dangerous one, at that.)

One further point needs to be made about White Noise. Before she assassinates him, Platonesse, who we have learned is a woman of color, addresses him as her "racist kindred." This again stresses that the evil she opposes, that we must oppose, is not separate from us but part of the cultural and human context we inhabit. However, there is a further reference which some may note: to Octavia Butler's novel *Kindred*. While there is much in that work I might wish to call readers' attention to, I at least want to note the possibility, which Platonesse suggests, that due to the rape endemic in American slavery, she and White Noise may be distantly related, even as they are clearly both part of the same human "family." White Noise of course, characteristically, denies that possibility. The irony here is not dramatic, but embedded in history itself.

If White Noise is the embodiment of hatred and avarice, it was obvious to me that Platonesse must be not only a woman, but a woman of color. Only she— or so the Chorus believes—

can slay the monster. And it is indeed a monster. This is why Platonesse must transform into The Final Girl. For those unfamiliar with horror film criticism, the "final girl" is a kind of archetype, the often terrified female subject in a horror film who, lacking male protection (often, after the male characters have either been killed or otherwise failed to arrive in her moment of danger), must face the monster alone, the evil (whether physical or supernatural), and vanquish it or at least outwit it to a degree that allows for her escape. My Final Girl is a reluctant hero, and indeed must be persuaded by the Chorus to take on this role, even as her friend Béranger has been captured by the Security Forces and is in what turns out to be grave danger. (Béranger's crime is that, like his namesake in the Ionesco play, he is a drunkard. This is said to make him "of a foreign nationality," which is an allusion to the film *Casablanca*, another touchstone antifascist work of art. In the film, Humphrey Bogart's character, Rick, is asked by the German major what his nationality is. Bogart's character cheekily replies, "I'm a drunkard.")

Some may be surprised at, for lack of a better word, the *sincerity* of some of the dialogue, especially in the final scenes. Yet while I admit that words like "truth" and "beauty," to name two, can have nuanced meanings dependent on historical and cultural (not to mention philosophical) contexts, here I felt a political urgency to prioritize clarity over ironic detachment, much less theoretical considerations. In a political and cultural climate in which truth is obscured for motives of power and greed, in which irony has been used to "soften" racism, xenophobia and misogyny, and in which so much drastically is at stake, it seems necessary to resort to sincerity, if that is the right word, as part of a language of refusal & resistance. This work is such an attempt.

While there are elements of farce, dramatic irony and absurdity at play here, this work is ultimately a tragedy. Yet it is a tragedy not only because of what happens at the very end; the tragedy (as Béranger, in his dying breath, prophesies) is the damage already done to our country and our culture. Thus, even as there is a note of hope struck in the Chorus's final speech, having once again found its courage after cowardly running away, much work still lies ahead of the surviving characters in this play, and of ourselves.

—Mark DuCharme
June, 2017

poetics and process: a conversation with mark ducharme and lynne desilva-johnson

Greetings comrade! Thank you for talking to us about your process today! Can you introduce yourself, in a way that you would choose?

I am a poet, an adjunct English professor at a community college, and an activist for faculty equity. I live in Boulder, am the author of a number of volumes of poetry including The Unfinished: Books I-VI *(2013), & hold an MFA from The Jack Kerouac School of Disembodied Poetics. And I absolutely hate beginning a lot of sentences with* I*! In fact, I think bios are overrated. The life is generally not as interesting as the work— unless either your work is particularly boring or your name is Arthur Rimbaud or Arthur Cravan. My name is not Arthur. But what do you think?*

Why are you a poet/writer/artist?

I don't think anyone (and especially someone who did not grow up well off) becomes a poet except out of a need to do so. I mean, it's not like choosing to become a doctor or plumber: it's impractical, perhaps glaringly so. But there's something beautiful & magical about inviting poetry into one's life. It is, or can be, a means through which one sees and encounters the world in previously unimaginable ways. Also, meeting other poets is usually pretty cool. I can't understand why everyone else doesn't do it.

When did you decide you were a poet/writer/artist (and/or: do you feel comfortable calling yourself a poet/writer/artist, what other titles or affiliations do you prefer/feel are more accurate)?

I knew that I must become an artist of some kind as a child. At first, I wasn't sure what kind. I was always a good expository writer in school, and one day, as a teenager, I was walking down Woodward Avenue in my hometown of Birmingham, Michigan with some friends, and we passed the Maximus & Company bookstore, which had just opened. (A great place, incidentally, run by poet Paul Lichter, which I would always visit when I returned to Birmingham to visit my mom. Among the volumes I bought there is Ted Berrigan's wonderful, and wonderfully titled, Nothing for You, *which, except for* The Sonnets, *is still my favorite Berrigan book.) In the storefront window that afternoon, the word POETRY was written in large letters. I looked across the street at it, and one of my friends quipped, "he's a poet." It felt right. I have never looked back.*

What's a "poet" (or "writer" or "artist") anyway?

Someone who writes poems. If you don't write poems, you can't call yourself a poet. This is something, by the way, that my first good creative writing teacher, Ken Mikolowski at the University of Michigan, said; I didn't come up with it, but I agree with him. I would add that a poet is, hopefully, someone whose poems do not suck.

What do you see as your cultural and social role (in the literary / artistic / creative community and beyond)?

One tries to write good poems and to neither bore oneself nor the reader. That is a valid cultural role in itself. Beyond that, I have been an editor & publisher (of photocopied microzines and better-produced chapbooks) and a reading series organizer. I am not currently doing anything of that sort, though I've thought about starting some sort of online journal. Maybe someday. However, I hasten to add that I am also a teacher, and while I don't currently teach creative writing, I feel that what I do is important (and time-consuming!) cultural work.

Talk about the process or instinct to move these poems (or your work in general) as independent entities into a body of work. How and why did this happen? Have you had this intention for a while? What encouraged and/or confounded this (or a book, in general) coming together? Was it a struggle?

In the summer of 2016, right around the time of the Republican National Convention (which is referenced in the text), I got the idea that maybe it would be interesting to write a "screenplay for an unrealizable film"— a work of indeterminate genre, as I conceived of it then. I had been writing almost exclusively what I call writing projects (my version of the serial poem, a term coined by Jack Spicer) for about a decade, and I felt it might be good to do something a little different. And I didn't have any idea what such a work would look like or if I could write it! (I had tried, unsuccessfully, to write a work of poet's theater when I was in my 20s.) So the whole thing was an experiment. I wrote a little bit of it that summer, but it was a "backburner" project at that point. Some of what I wrote then didn't end up making it into the final manuscript.

Then, something I didn't anticipate ended up happening: Donald Trump won the presidential election. I felt, as I'm sure you did, a mixture of despair and outrage and shocked incredulity. I was utterly horrified. The first thing I think I wrote then— though I may also have been working to an extent on We, the Monstrous *while I was writing this— was a sequence of poems called "American Dirge," none of which have yet been published. The tone of that sequence is essentially mournful, reflecting my initial shock & despair. At some point, the mourning if not the other feelings dropped away, & my attention turned to what became* We, the Monstrous. *I developed a working title,* White Noise vs. The Final Girl, *and I started more seriously to try to develop this work. I even told some friends I was working on it. By June— just less than a year after I had gotten the vague, initial idea— I had the completed and revised manuscript, which I then submitted to you.*

What formal structures or other constrictive practices (if any) do you use in the creation of your work?

I don't tend to use constrictive practices (e.g., Oulipian procedures). I write intuitively. I have written sometimes in poetic forms, though. I have one sestina that I still very much like ("A World," in my 2002 book Cosmopolitan Tremble). *I have "Two Villanelles" in my book* Answer *(2011). I have written acrostics, and I seem to be good at pantoums.*

Have certain teachers or instructive environments, or readings/writings/work of other creative people informed the way you work/write?

I am going to interpret this question as being about influence and lineage. Many poets' work has informed my practice, and there are many poets whose work I admire. I am always reading different poets, though I also reread those whose work is especially important to me. Frank O'Hara was an early, important influence. Thus, Ted Berrigan, Ron Padgett, and later Joseph Ceravolo became key influences as well. Other poets whose work I admire and have been informed by include (in no particular order) Clark Coolidge, César Vallejo, Pierre Reverdy, John Ashbery, Robert Creeley, Alice Notley, Gertrude Stein, Guillaume Apollinaire, Emily Dickinson, Barbara Guest, Lorine Niedecker, Arthur Rimbaud, Charles Baudelaire, Jack Spicer, Jackson Mac Low, Bernadette Mayer, Stephen Rodefer, Michael Gizzi, George Oppen, Mina Loy, William Carlos Williams, Maureen Owen, Anselm Hollo— I could go on.

Speaking of monikers, what does your title represent? How was it generated? Talk about the way you titled the book, and how your process of naming (individual pieces, sections, etc) influences you and/or colors your work specifically.

I decided that I didn't want to use White Noise vs. The Final Girl, *which had been the working title during most of the writing process, because I felt it simplified the issues the work addresses & perhaps gave away a key plot development which takes place in the long final scene of Act III. Therefore, I needed another title. Titles for books can be a sticky point for me, or they can come very easily— it just depends. In this case, once I rejected the working title, I don't recall it being a long or arduous process to come up with another I thought better represented this work. Though the phrase itself doesn't appear in the text,* We, the Monstrous *comes from an exchange between my protagonist Platonesse (speaking here as She) and Béranger (speaking here as He):*

> HE: The oppressors do not change.
> They remain an image of the monstrous.
>
> SHE: No, they are an image of
> *Ourselves*— of what humanity,
> Our *species*,
> Is capable of doing.
> Humans behave inhumanly

> Inhu*m*a*nely, instinctively, & then define*
> Ourselves, a species, as
> The opposite of all our actions.

Obviously, when I wrote We, the Monstrous *I was thinking a lot about how so many American voters could have voted for a man who represented so clearly, in my mind, a renewal of hatred, prejudice, class privilege (thinly disguised as populism), misogyny and racism— a figure who seemed and still seems to threaten fascism, and who, politics aside, is so obviously unfit for the highest office in the land that he constitutes a public danger. But my notion of the inhumanity of humans also stems from my knowledge of the historical Romans, the Crusades, "witch" burnings, American slavery, the Trail of Tears, the rise of the KKK, early & violent repression of union organizing, the Holocaust (among other genocides), lynchings in the American south, US militarism & interventions, etc. The term "monster," incidentally, also appears in my "American Dirge" sequence, mentioned earlier.*

What does this particular work represent to you as indicative of your method/creative practice, your history, your mission/intentions/hopes/plans?

Despite its subtitle, I very much consider We, the Monstrous *a poem at least as much as a dramatic work. I currently have no plans to write another dramatic work. Right now, I am working on a collection of poems.*

What does this book DO (as much as what it says or contains)?

Hopefully, it achieves both its poetic and political aims.

What would be the best possible outcome for this book? What might it do in the world, and how will its presence as an object facilitate your creative role in your community and beyond? What are your hopes for this book, and for your practice?

The best possible outcome for this book would be to find readers, to make them think, to make them feel, and to change the way they may encounter/ interact with the political/ poetic landscape, however defined. More specifically, another best possible outcome would be to aid & inspire the current resistance to this abomination of an administration, this rampant kleptocracy, this oligarchy de luxe. In terms of my role in my community, I'd love to do a staged reading if I could cast all the roles. If anyone reading this lives in Colorado and wants to play Platonesse or knows someone who would be a good Platonesse, contact me. I would also be open to staged readings or productions of the work in other parts of the country.

Let's talk a little bit about the role of poetics and creative community in social activism, in particular in what I call "Civil Rights 2.0," which has remained immediately present all around us in the time leading up to this series' publication. I'd be curious to hear some thoughts on the challenges we face in speaking and publishing across lines of race, age, privilege, social/cultural background, and sexuality within the community, vs. the dangers of remaining and producing in isolated "silos."

Well, poetry is a "silo," isn't it? And I don't mean just "avant-garde" poetry, so called, of which I consider my body of work a part, but even that mundane, sometimes maudlin poetry promoted by Ted Kooser and others that is supposed to be the sort of poetry that will finally appeal to the majority of readers(!), if only the more vital and interesting, but (necessarily) challenging, poetry would just get out of the way. (And what's next: glossy regional poetry anthologies in the check-out aisles?)

There are the "silos" of progressive, liberal, conservative and reactionary politics, there is the poetry silo, and then there are the silos you refer to. As writers whose identities are defined in privileged way(s)— in any of the ways you mention— it is incumbent on us to check our privilege at the door. There is no single recipe for doing this, and no one can claim perfection in that regard, but as humans we have to try. And the most important thing we can do, I think, is support others of differing backgrounds/ statuses, be genuine, and listen *rather than doing all the speaking.*

Look, we all live in silos of one kind or another. As a poet, I live in my head. But, just like you don't stay in your room all day, hopefully, it need not be a question of where you "live" so much as whether you go out, & where.

Get off Facebook *and other social media, which, other than cliques, are probably the biggest "silos" of all. I am on FB, but I try, not always successfully, to limit my time there. Get out in the community (ironic for me to say, because I'm such an introvert). Move outside your comfort zone, & question your assumptions. Challenge bullshit when you hear it, especially in real life. Do not think that online forums "count" as real life. Question authority, as one used to say, & be not docile. Read a lot & inform yourself. Be aware of what is going on in your community, even if you cannot always attend everything. Attend what you can, & do what you can. If you teach, do not be didactic, but try to provoke students to think in ways they might not have expected. Be a real human being; be considerate & kind. Cultivate empathy & compassion— so lacking in these crazy times! These things are all part of being a poet.*

Is there anything else we should have asked, or that you want to share?

Thank you!

Part of this work appeared in *Dispatches from the Poetry Wars*.
Thanks to editors Kent Johnson and Michael Boughn.

MARK DuCHARME's books of poetry include *The Unfinished: Books I-VI* (2013), *Answer* (2011) and *The Sensory Cabinet* (2007). Most recently, *Counter Fluencies 1-20* appeared as part of the print journal *The Lune* (2017). His poetry has appeared widely in such publications as *Big Bridge, Bombay Gin, Caliban Online, Colorado Review, Mantis, New American Writing, OR, Pallaksch Pallaksch, Shiny, Talisman, and Vanitas*. He has been a recipient of the Neodata Endowment in Literature and the Gertrude Stein Award in Innovative American Poetry. He lives in Boulder, Colorado.

WHY PRINT DOCUMENT?

The Operating System uses the language "print document" to differentiate from the book-object as part of our mission to distinguish the act of documentation-in-book-FORM from the act of publishing as a backwards-facing replication of the book's agentive *role* as it may have appeared the last several centuries of its history. Ultimately, I approach the book as TECHNOLOGY: one of a variety of printed documents (in this case, bound*) that humans have invented and in turn used to archive and disseminate ideas, beliefs, stories, and other evidence of production.*

Ownership and use of printing presses and access to (or restriction of printed materials) has long been a site of struggle, related in many ways to revolutionary activity and the fight for civil rights and free speech all over the world. While (in many countries) the contemporary quotidian landscape has indeed drastically shifted in its access to platforms for sharing information and in the widespread ability to "publish" digitally, even with extremely limited resources, the importance of publication on physical media has not diminished. In fact, this may be the most critical time in recent history for activist groups, artists, and others to insist upon learning, establishing, and encouraging personal and community documentation practices. Hear me out.

With The OS's print endeavors I wanted to open up a conversation about this: the ultimately radical, transgressive act of creating PRINT /DOCUMENTATION in the digital age. It's a question of the archive, and of history: who gets to tell the story, and what evidence of our life, our behaviors, our experiences are we leaving behind? We can know little to nothing about the future into which we're leaving an unprecedentedly digital document trail — but we can be assured that publications, government agencies, museums, schools, and other institutional powers that be will continue to leave BOTH a digital and print version of their production for the official record. Will we?

As a (rogue) anthropologist and long time academic, I can easily pull up many accounts about how lives, behaviors, experiences — how THE STORY of a time or place — was pieced together using the deep study of correspondence, notebooks, and other physical documents which are no longer the norm in many lives and practices. As we move our creative behaviors towards digital note taking, and even audio and video, what can we predict about future technology that is in any way assuring that our stories will be accurately told – or told at all? How will we leave these things for the record?

In these documents we say: WE WERE HERE, WE EXISTED, WE HAVE A DIFFERENT STORY

- Lynne DeSilva-Johnson, Founder/Managing Editor,
THE OPERATING SYSTEM, Brooklyn NY 2017

SELECTED RECENT AND FORTHCOMING OS PRINT/DOCUMENTS

Ark Hive-Marthe Reed [2019]
A Bony Framework for the Tangible Universe-D. Allen [kin(d)*, 2019]
Śnienie / Dreaming - Marta Zelwan/Krystyna Sakowicz,
(Polish-English/dual-language) trans. Victoria Miluch [glossarium, 2019]
Opera on TV-James Brunton [kin(d)*, 2019]
Alparegho: Pareil-À-Rien / Alparegho, Like Nothing Else - Hélène Sanguinetti
(French-English/dual-language), trans. Ann Cefola [glossarium, 2019]
Hall of Waters-Berry Grass [kin(d)*, 2019]
High Tide Of The Eyes - Bijan Elahi (Farsi-English/dual-language)
trans. Rebecca Ruth Gould and Kayvan Tahmasebian [glossarium, 2019]
I Made for You a New Machine and All it Does is Hope - Richard Lucyshyn [2019]
Illusory Borders-Heidi Reszies [2019]
Transitional Object-Adrian Silbernagel [kin(d)*, 2019]
A Year of Misreading the Wildcats [2019]

An Absence So Great and Spontaneous It Is Evidence of Light - Anne Gorrick [2018]
The Book of Everyday Instruction - Chloe Bass [2018]
Executive Orders Vol. II - a collaboration with the Organism for Poetic Research [2018]
One More Revolution - Andrea Mazzariello [2018]
The Suitcase Tree - Filip Marinovich [2018]
Chlorosis - Michael Flatt and Derrick Mund [2018]
Sussuros a Mi Padre - Erick Sáenz [2018]
Sharing Plastic - Blake Nemec [2018]
The Book of Sounds - Mehdi Navid (Farsi dual language, trans. Tina Rahimi) [2018]
In Corpore Sano : Creative Practice and the Challenged Body [Anthology, 2018];
Lynne DeSilva-Johnson and Jay Besemer, co-editors
Abandoners - Lesley Ann Wheeler [2018]
Jazzercise is a Language - Gabriel Ojeda-Sague [2018]
Return Trip / Viaje Al Regreso - Israel Dominguez;
(Spanish-English dual language) trans. Margaret Randall [2018]
Born Again - Ivy Johnson [2018]
Attendance - Rocío Carlos and Rachel McLeod Kaminer [2018]
Singing for Nothing - Wally Swist [2018]
The Ways of the Monster - Jay Besemer [2018]
Walking Away From Explosions in Slow Motion - Gregory Crosby [2018]
The Unspoken - Bob Holman [Bowery Books imprint - 2018]
Field Guide to Autobiography - Melissa Eleftherion [2018]
Kawsay: The Flame of the Jungle - María Vázquez Valdez
(Spanish-English dual language) trans. Margaret Randall [2018]

OS PRINT DOCUMENT ANNUAL CHAPBOOK SERIES TITLES

CHAPBOOK SERIES 2018 : TALES
Greater Grave - Jacq Greyja; Needles of Itching Feathers - Jared Schlickling;
Want-Catcher - Adra Raine; We, The Monstrous - Mark DuCharme

CHAPBOOK SERIES 2017 : INCANTATIONS
featuring original cover art by Barbara Byers
sp. - Susan Charkes; Radio Poems - Jeffrey Cyphers Wright;
Fixing a Witch/Hexing the Stitch - Jacklyn Janeksela;
cosmos a personal voyage by carl sagan ann druyan steven sotor and me - Connie Mae Oliver

CHAPBOOK SERIES 2016: OF SOUND MIND
*featuring the quilt drawings of Daphne Taylor
Improper Maps - Alex Crowley; While Listening - Alaina Ferris;
Chords - Peter Longofono; Any Seam or Needlework - Stanford Cheung

CHAPBOOK SERIES 2015: OF SYSTEMS OF
*featuring original cover art by Emma Steinkraus
Cyclorama - Davy Knittle; The Sensitive Boy Slumber Party Manifesto - Joseph Cuillier; Neptune Court - Anton Yakovlev; Schema - Anurak Saelow

CHAPBOOK SERIES 2014: BY HAND
Pull, A Ballad - Maryam Parhizkar;
Can You See that Sound - Jeff Musillo
Executive Producer Chris Carter - Peter Milne Greiner;
Spooky Action at a Distance - Gregory Crosby;

CHAPBOOK SERIES 2013: WOODBLOCK
*featuring original prints from Kevin William Reed
Strange Coherence - Bill Considine; The Sword of Things - Tony Hoffman;
Talk About Man Proof - Lancelot Runge / John Kropa;
An Admission as a Warning Against the Value of Our Conclusions -Alexis Quinlan

DOC U MENT
/däkyəmənt/

First meant "instruction" or "evidence," whether written or not.

noun - a piece of written, printed, or electronic matter that provides information or evidence or that serves as an official record
verb - record (something) in written, photographic, or other form
synonyms - paper - deed - record - writing - act - instrument

[Middle English, precept, from Old French, from Latin *documentum*, example, proof, from *docre*, to teach; see *dek-* in Indo-European roots.]

Who is responsible for the manufacture of value?

Based on what supercilious ontology have we landed in a space where we vie against other creative people in vain pursuit of the fleeting credibilities of the scarcity economy, rather than freely collaborating and sharing openly with each other in ecstatic celebration of MAKING?

While we understand and acknowledge the economic pressures and fear-mongering that threatens to dominate and crush the creative impulse, we also believe that **now more than ever we have the tools to relinquish agency via cooperative means,** fueled by the fires of the Open Source Movement.

Looking out across the invisible vistas of that rhizomatic parallel country we can begin to see our community beyond constraints, in the place where intention meets resilient, proactive, collaborative organization.

Here is a document born of that belief, sown purely of imagination and will.
When we document we assert. We print to make real, to reify our being there.
When we do so with mindful intention to address our process, to open our work to others, to create beauty in words in space, to respect and acknowledge the strength of the page we now hold physical, a thing in our hand… we remind ourselves that, like Dorothy: *we had the power all along, my dears.*

THE PRINT! DOCUMENT SERIES

is a project of
the trouble with bartleby
in collaboration with
the operating system

www.ingramcontent.com/pod-product-compliance
Lightning Source LLC
Chambersburg PA
CBHW081339080526
44588CB00017B/2678